GAMES FOR
Baby Shower Fun

By Sharon Dlugosch

Illustrations by Sandra Knuth

Copyright © 1987 by Sharon E. Dlugosch

Brighton Publications, Inc.
P.O. Box 120706
New Brighton, MN 55112
(612) 636-2220

First Edition: 1987
Reprint: 1990, 1991, 1993, 1993, 1995

Printed in the United States of America
Library of Congress Catalog
Card Number: 83-073599
International Standard Book Number
0-918420-20-2

Contents

Welcome to the World of Baby Showers!

What's new in the world of baby showers? Plenty! Here you'll find a sprinkling of new game ideas, creative memory-makers to make your shower a bit different from any other, door prizes as a way of saying thank you to your guests, and four ready-to-go, tear-out game sheets for up to twelve guests each. In addition, there is a prize guide featuring prize ideas as well as suggestions on ways to present them, and name tag patterns.

You're guaranteed to find shower ideas and games for to-day's life styles, including the growing trend of couples showers. Select just a few ideas and games or use them all to make your shower a fun occasion for everyone to enjoy.

Door Prize Fun

For a change of pace, let's focus our gift attention on the guests with door prize setups. Door prizes allow you to present surprise gifts to your guests just for attending your shower and helping to make happy memories for the guest of honor. You can use as many of these ideas as you wish. In fact, you may use them all, each at a different moment in the shower. Because they'll add sparkle and variety, you'll want to do it with flair. A drum roll, piano chord, or bell will alert your guests to the coming excitement.

For the Alphabet Choice drawing, you will need name tags. Name tag patterns are provided after the tear-out game sheet section. After cutting out, write a letter of the alphabet on each name tag. At the shower, simply have guests write their names on the tags and pin or tape them on.

Alphabet Choice

Display children's alphabet blocks in a glass fishbowl or a large brandy snifter. Before the shower, add a letter to each name tag and mark an "X" on just one side of each block to indicate a letter choice. Use washable ink on the blocks so the markings won't be permanent. When it's door prize time, ask the guest of honor to draw a block and announce the winning letter. Continue until all the prizes have been awarded. After the shower, the alphabet blocks can be given to the guest of honor.

"Thank You Notes" Drawing

Purchase thank you notes. As guests are writing their names on name tags ask them to address an envelope to themselves. Collect the envelopes and stand them upright in a snug-fitting box. When the time is appropriate for giving the door prize, the guest of honor can pull out an envelope and read the name. You can give one grand prize or several small door prizes with this method. The guest of honor will automatically win the thank you notes as a door prize. It goes without saying that the job of writing thank yous will be a lot easier for the guest of honor using this door prize setup.

Sticker Surprise!

Put a sticker representing your shower theme under chairs, plates, or cups for some serious door prize doings. A bear, balloon, shower umbrella, or any other colorful sticker will tell who the winner of the next door prize will be. Feature door prize drawings intermittently throughout the shower to keep everyone in a winning frame of mind.

Game Sprinkles

Keep your shower going with more game ideas. These fun and easy-to-use games will perk up any shower with just a little pre-party planning by you.

What's in a Nickname!

Nicknames can be attention getters; perhaps that's why they are easy to remember. But can you remember the proper names? Choose fifteen to twenty famous nicknames and ask your guests to give the matching proper name. If you have guests with nicknames, add them to the list as well. Give a prize to the person with the most correct answers. Here are a few examples to get you started: Bubbles (Beverly Sills), Rough Rider (Theodore Roosevelt), Happy (Margretta Rockefeller), Flip (Clerow Wilson), Lady Bird (Claudia Alta Johnson), Lucky Lindy (Charles Lindbergh).

Nursery Rhyme Acronyms

Form a sequence of letters to make informal acronyms of first lines of well-known nursery rhymes. Write the acronyms on slips of paper and fold. Put them all together on a plate and ask each guest to draw a slip. Each person writes the answer to their acronym on a separate sheet of paper and then, at a signal, passes the acronym on to his or her neighbor. The person who has the most correct answers wins the prize.

Here is an example: HDSOAW

Answer: Humpty Dumpty sat on a wall

How-To Toy Challenge

Fisher-Price and Kenner Toys, watch out! There is no telling what will happen when you divide the group into two-person teams and challenge them to create a toy with the material at hand. Scour craft stores and dime stores for building materials such as wheels, balsa wood pieces, dowels, colored paper, fabric, string, watercolors, and crayons. Offer one prize each for the most colorful, the most imaginative, and the easiest-to-make toy. This contest is certain to bring out the child in everyone.

Name the Baby Brands

Test your guest's knowledge of popular baby brands. Find ten to fifteen well-known baby products with identifiable slogans or logos. Do these sound familiar?

The perfect name for baby _____

    Answer: Carter's

The most trusted name in fever relief _____

    Answer: Children's Tylenol

Babies are our business _____

    Answer: Gerber

. . . to help stop leaking_____

    Answer: Kleenex Huggies

Read the clues out loud or show the logos to your audience. Ask them to choose the correct answers from a list of possible answers displayed in the room. The best pay-attention consumer in the group wins a prize.

Reach for the Stars

Do you want your guests to leave your shower with the feeling that this was the best party ever? Then focus a little star quality attention on each guest. Collect baby pictures of everyone and mix them together. Award a prize to the guest who is quickest in matching the right baby picture to each guest. Only one person wins, but everyone gets to star in this game.

Memory-Makers

While games are fun, these memory makers will add a new dimension to your shower. Sometimes their intent is to recall the past . . . sometimes to start a new tradition . . . and every time to create deep down, lasting memories.

Tablecloth Design

Purchase a white tablecloth and a good selection of colored permanent markers or textile pens. In the center of the cloth write baby's name, birth date, and parent's name. Decorate this information and the corners and edges of the tablecloth with swirls, flowers, stars, and so on. Once the shower begins, ask your guests to write out a wish for the new baby and to sign their names. Leave as is, or embroider the signatures and decorative markings after the shower. This tablecloth can then be used and signed at subsequent birthday parties.

What's In, What's Out?

Ask your guests to make two lists. For the first one ask them to list things that will be only a passing memory, and in the second list ask for things that will still be around in the year 2010! Gather the completed lists and after sharing everyones' ideas, place the lists in an envelope. The envelope should read, "For Baby – To Be Opened January 1, 2010!"

Baby Fashion

Fashion a display from the baby wardrobes of the new parents and perhaps of the grandparents, too. Ask for any christening dresses, bronzed shoes, jewelry, silver spoons, or comb and brush sets. Label and display each item.

Comfort Kit

Help the new parents prepare for their bundle-of-love challenge with a survival kit. Ask each guest to bring one item to help the new parents through those first months of child care. A flashlight, snuggly slippers, a Brahms lullaby tape, packets of hot chocolate, a roll of Life Savers, a baby pacifier, and aspirin with a note and signature will be welcome reminders later on of the baby shower given in their honor.

History in the Making

Too many times we get the historians viewpoint (read that "impersonal history") of the year that was. Let's give the new baby your personal on the scene judgement of what really was important during baby's birth year. This will be a written record of what you feel to be important in business, science, medicine, sports, entertainment, and personal family and friend affairs.

Prize Guide

Prizes can range from the practical to the whimsical. Somehow, what you win never seems to matter as much as that you do win something. So, rather then spending the whole prize budget on one or two fabulous items, buy enough prizes to make everyone feel like a winner.

You can add extra spirit and vitality to the prize-giving event by presenting the prizes in style. Tuck prizes into a child's sand pail, a plastic boat or truck, the arms of a plush bear, or a bright paper bag and tissue. If you wrap the prize, use bright colored paper or cellophane, and top off the package with a big satin bow or blown-up balloon.

Prize Suggestions

Kaleidoscope, magnifying glass, phone number/address book, letter opener, personal diary, pencil sharpener, stamp dispenser, note cards, appointment book, calender, pencil holder, letter holder.

Coffee mug, set of paper napkins, wooden cooking utensil, napkins, how-to napkin folding book, printed shopping list pad, recipe box, refrigerator magnets, mesh basket, bone china cup and saucer.

Small tin box, decorative candle, playing cards, picture frame, photo book, novelty stickers, key chain holder, earring organizer, change holder, straw basket, novelty tray, cloth wine tote, bottle recorker, long-stemmed chocolate rose, jack-in-the-box toy.

House plant, packets of herb, flower, or vegetable seeds, house plant tool kit, outdoor thermometer, small birdfeeder, windsock, inflatable pool accessories.

Ready-to-Use Games

You'll find four new hassle-free games on the following pages, with game sheets for twelve guests each. Simply tear along the perforations and pass them out. Set your own time limit on the games that require one. Answers can be found on pages 110-111.

Famous Baby Trivia

Put on your thinking bonnet and name these babies. Some are real and some are from the movies, some are treasured tales and some are just loved. Anyone who guesses the most babies wins the game.

1. A "dear" creature of the forest _____

2. Flintstone's chip off the old block _____

3. World's youngest cynic _____

4. A biblical basket case _____

5. Bumstead's sweet dough _____

6. All ears_____

7. Devil may care _____

8. A fresh start _____

9. A fowl inspiration _____

10. Lots of sparkle in a comic strip _____

11. Honey child _____

12. Bette Davis won an Academy award nomination for this

    picture _____

13. Rocking tune _____

14. The apple of Pop's eye _____

15. A soft touch_____

Famous Baby Trivia

Put on your thinking bonnet and name these babies. Some are real and some are from the movies, some are treasured tales and some are just loved. Anyone who guesses the most babies wins the game.

1. A "dear" creature of the forest _____

2. Flintstone's chip off the old block _____

3. World's youngest cynic _____

4. A biblical basket case _____

5. Bumstead's sweet dough _____

6. All ears_____

7. Devil may care _____

8. A fresh start _____

9. A fowl inspiration _____

10. Lots of sparkle in a comic strip _____

11. Honey child _____

12. Bette Davis won an Academy award nomination for this

   picture _____

13. Rocking tune _____

14. The apple of Pop's eye _____

15. A soft touch_____

© 1987, BRIGHTON PUBLICATIONS, INC.

Famous Baby Trivia

Put on your thinking bonnet and name these babies. Some are real and some are from the movies, some are treasured tales and some are just loved. Anyone who guesses the most babies wins the game.

1. A "dear" creature of the forest _____

2. Flintstone's chip off the old block _____

3. World's youngest cynic _____

4. A biblical basket case _____

5. Bumstead's sweet dough _____

6. All ears _____

7. Devil may care _____

8. A fresh start _____

9. A fowl inspiration _____

10. Lots of sparkle in a comic strip _____

11. Honey child _____

12. Bette Davis won an Academy award nomination for this

    picture _____

13. Rocking tune _____

14. The apple of Pop's eye _____

15. A soft touch _____

© 1987, BRIGHTON PUBLICATIONS, INC.

Famous Baby Trivia

Put on your thinking bonnet and name these babies. Some are real and some are from the movies, some are treasured tales and some are just loved. Anyone who guesses the most babies wins the game.

1. A "dear" creature of the forest _____

2. Flintstone's chip off the old block _____

3. World's youngest cynic _____

4. A biblical basket case _____

5. Bumstead's sweet dough _____

6. All ears_____

7. Devil may care _____

8. A fresh start _____

9. A fowl inspiration _____

10. Lots of sparkle in a comic strip _____

11. Honey child _____

12. Bette Davis won an Academy award nomination for this picture _____

13. Rocking tune _____

14. The apple of Pop's eye _____

15. A soft touch_____

Famous Baby Trivia

Put on your thinking bonnet and name these babies. Some are real and some are from the movies, some are treasured tales and some are just loved. Anyone who guesses the most babies wins the game.

1. A "dear" creature of the forest _____

2. Flintstone's chip off the old block _____

3. World's youngest cynic _____

4. A biblical basket case _____

5. Bumstead's sweet dough _____

6. All ears_____

7. Devil may care _____

8. A fresh start _____

9. A fowl inspiration _____

10. Lots of sparkle in a comic strip _____

11. Honey child _____

12. Bette Davis won an Academy award nomination for this

    picture _____

13. Rocking tune _____

14. The apple of Pop's eye _____

15. A soft touch_____

© 1987, BRIGHTON PUBLICATIONS, INC.

Famous Baby Trivia

Put on your thinking bonnet and name these babies. Some are real and some are from the movies, some are treasured tales and some are just loved. Anyone who guesses the most babies wins the game.

1. A "dear" creature of the forest _____

2. Flintstone's chip off the old block _____

3. World's youngest cynic _____

4. A biblical basket case _____

5. Bumstead's sweet dough _____

6. All ears_____

7. Devil may care _____

8. A fresh start _____

9. A fowl inspiration _____

10. Lots of sparkle in a comic strip _____

11. Honey child _____

12. Bette Davis won an Academy award nomination for this

    picture _____

13. Rocking tune _____

14. The apple of Pop's eye _____

15. A soft touch_____

Famous Baby Trivia

Put on your thinking bonnet and name these babies. Some are real and some are from the movies, some are treasured tales and some are just loved. Anyone who guesses the most babies wins the game.

1. A "dear" creature of the forest _____

2. Flintstone's chip off the old block _____

3. World's youngest cynic _____

4. A biblical basket case _____

5. Bumstead's sweet dough _____

6. All ears_____

7. Devil may care _____

8. A fresh start _____

9. A fowl inspiration _____

10. Lots of sparkle in a comic strip _____

11. Honey child _____

12. Bette Davis won an Academy award nomination for this

   picture _____

13. Rocking tune _____

14. The apple of Pop's eye _____

15. A soft touch_____

© 1987, BRIGHTON PUBLICATIONS, INC.

Famous Baby Trivia

Put on your thinking bonnet and name these babies. Some are real and some are from the movies, some are treasured tales and some are just loved. Anyone who guesses the most babies wins the game.

1. A "dear" creature of the forest _____

2. Flintstone's chip off the old block _____

3. World's youngest cynic _____

4. A biblical basket case _____

5. Bumstead's sweet dough _____

6. All ears _____

7. Devil may care _____

8. A fresh start _____

9. A fowl inspiration _____

10. Lots of sparkle in a comic strip _____

11. Honey child _____

12. Bette Davis won an Academy award nomination for this

    picture _____

13. Rocking tune _____

14. The apple of Pop's eye _____

15. A soft touch _____

© 1987, BRIGHTON PUBLICATIONS, INC.

Famous Baby Trivia

Put on your thinking bonnet and name these babies. Some are real and some are from the movies, some are treasured tales and some are just loved. Anyone who guesses the most babies wins the game.

1. A "dear" creature of the forest _____

2. Flintstone's chip off the old block _____

3. World's youngest cynic _____

4. A biblical basket case _____

5. Bumstead's sweet dough _____

6. All ears_____

7. Devil may care _____

8. A fresh start _____

9. A fowl inspiration _____

10. Lots of sparkle in a comic strip _____

11. Honey child _____

12. Bette Davis won an Academy award nomination for this

    picture _____

13. Rocking tune _____

14. The apple of Pop's eye _____

15. A soft touch_____

Famous Baby Trivia

Put on your thinking bonnet and name these babies. Some are real and some are from the movies, some are treasured tales and some are just loved. Anyone who guesses the most babies wins the game.

1. A "dear" creature of the forest _____

2. Flintstone's chip off the old block _____

3. World's youngest cynic _____

4. A biblical basket case _____

5. Bumstead's sweet dough _____

6. All ears _____

7. Devil may care _____

8. A fresh start _____

9. A fowl inspiration _____

10. Lots of sparkle in a comic strip _____

11. Honey child _____

12. Bette Davis won an Academy award nomination for this

    picture _____

13. Rocking tune _____

14. The apple of Pop's eye _____

15. A soft touch _____

© 1987, BRIGHTON PUBLICATIONS, INC.

Famous Baby Trivia

Put on your thinking bonnet and name these babies. Some are real and some are from the movies, some are treasured tales and some are just loved. Anyone who guesses the most babies wins the game.

1. A "dear" creature of the forest _____

2. Flintstone's chip off the old block _____

3. World's youngest cynic _____

4. A biblical basket case _____

5. Bumstead's sweet dough _____

6. All ears_____

7. Devil may care _____

8. A fresh start _____

9. A fowl inspiration _____

10. Lots of sparkle in a comic strip _____

11. Honey child_____

12. Bette Davis won an Academy award nomination for this

    picture _____

13. Rocking tune _____

14. The apple of Pop's eye _____

15. A soft touch_____

Famous Baby Trivia

Put on your thinking bonnet and name these babies. Some are real and some are from the movies, some are treasured tales and some are just loved. Anyone who guesses the most babies wins the game.

1. A "dear" creature of the forest _____

2. Flintstone's chip off the old block _____

3. World's youngest cynic _____

4. A biblical basket case _____

5. Bumstead's sweet dough _____

6. All ears_____

7. Devil may care _____

8. A fresh start _____

9. A fowl inspiration _____

10. Lots of sparkle in a comic strip _____

11. Honey child _____

12. Bette Davis won an Academy award nomination for this

     picture _____

13. Rocking tune _____

14. The apple of Pop's eye _____

15. A soft touch_____

© 1987, BRIGHTON PUBLICATIONS, INC.

"B" is for Baby

By adding B's to the letters below, you will create first lines of well-known Mother Goose Rhymes. Each sequence of letters ends with the number of B's required. The first guest to fill in all the lines correctly is the winner. So get set . . . ready . . . go!

1. littleoylue (2) _____

2. ruadudu (3) _____

3. aaaalacksheep (3) _____

4. lowwindlow (2) _____

5. owwowwow (1) _____

6. yeayunting (4) _____

7. colercolermendmyshoe (4) _____

8. hotcrossunshotcrossuns (2) _____

9. hushayeayonthetreetop (3) _____

10. ladyirdladyird (2) _____

"B" is for Baby

By adding B's to the letters below, you will create first lines of well-known Mother Goose Rhymes. Each sequence of letters ends with the number of B's required. The first guest to fill in all the lines correctly is the winner. So get set . . . ready . . . go!

1. littleoylue (2) _____

2. ruadudu (3) _____

3. aaaalacksheep (3) _____

4. lowwindlow (2) _____

5. owwowwow (1) _____

6. yeayunting (4) _____

7. colercolermendmyshoe (4) _____

8. hotcrossunshotcrossuns (2) _____

9. hushayeayonthetreetop (3) _____

10. ladyirdladyird (2) _____

"B" is for Baby

By adding B's to the letters below, you will create first lines of well-known Mother Goose Rhymes. Each sequence of letters ends with the number of B's required. The first guest to fill in all the lines correctly is the winner. So get set . . . ready . . . go!

1. littleoylue (2) _____

2. ruadudu (3) _____

3. aaaalacksheep (3) _____

4. lowwindlow (2) _____

5. owwowwow (1) _____

6. yeayunting (4) _____

7. colercolermendmyshoe (4) _____

8. hotcrossunshotcrossuns (2) _____

9. hushayeayonthetreetop (3) _____

10. ladyirdladyird (2) _____

"B" is for Baby

By adding B's to the letters below, you will create first lines of well-known Mother Goose Rhymes. Each sequence of letters ends with the number of B's required. The first guest to fill in all the lines correctly is the winner. So get set . . . ready . . . go!

1. littleoylue (2) _____

2. ruadudu (3) _____

3. aaaalacksheep (3) _____

4. lowwindlow (2) _____

5. owwowwow (1) _____

6. yeayunting (4) _____

7. colercolermendmyshoe (4)_____

8. hotcrossunshotcrossuns (2) _____

9. hushayeayonthetreetop (3) _____

10. ladyirdladyird (2) _____

"B" is for Baby

By adding B's to the letters below, you will create first lines of well-known Mother Goose Rhymes. Each sequence of letters ends with the number of B's required. The first guest to fill in all the lines correctly is the winner. So get set . . . ready . . . go!

1. littleoylue (2) _____

2. ruadudu (3) _____

3. aaaalacksheep (3) _____

4. lowwindlow (2) _____

5. owwowwow (1) _____

6. yeayunting (4) _____

7. colercolermendmyshoe (4) _____

8. hotcrossunshotcrossuns (2) _____

9. hushayeayonthetreetop (3) _____

10. ladyirdladyird (2) _____

"B" is for Baby

By adding B's to the letters below, you will create first lines of well-known Mother Goose Rhymes. Each sequence of letters ends with the number of B's required. The first guest to fill in all the lines correctly is the winner. So get set . . . ready . . . go!

1. littleoylue (2) _____

2. ruadudu (3) _____

3. aaaalacksheep (3) _____

4. lowwindlow (2) _____

5. owwowwow (1) _____

6. yeayunting (4) _____

7. colercolermendmyshoe (4) _____

8. hotcrossunshotcrossuns (2) _____

9. hushayeayonthetreetop (3) _____

10. ladyirdladyird (2) _____

"B" is for Baby

By adding B's to the letters below, you will create first lines of well-known Mother Goose Rhymes. Each sequence of letters ends with the number of B's required. The first guest to fill in all the lines correctly is the winner. So get set . . . ready . . . go!

1. littleoylue (2) _____

2. ruadudu (3) _____

3. aaaalacksheep (3) _____

4. lowwindlow (2) _____

5. owwowwow (1) _____

6. yeayunting (4) _____

7. colercolermendmyshoe (4) _____

8. hotcrossunshotcrossuns (2) _____

9. hushayeayonthetreetop (3) _____

10. ladyirdladyird (2) _____

"B" is for Baby

By adding B's to the letters below, you will create first lines of well-known Mother Goose Rhymes. Each sequence of letters ends with the number of B's required. The first guest to fill in all the lines correctly is the winner. So get set . . . ready . . . go!

1. littleoylue (2) _____

2. ruadudu (3) _____

3. aaaalacksheep (3) _____

4. lowwindlow (2) _____

5. owwowwow (1) _____

6. yeayunting (4) _____

7. colercolermendmyshoe (4) _____

8. hotcrossunshotcrossuns (2) _____

9. hushayeayonthetreetop (3) _____

10. ladyirdladyird (2) _____

"B" is for Baby

By adding B's to the letters below, you will create first lines of well-known Mother Goose Rhymes. Each sequence of letters ends with the number of B's required. The first guest to fill in all the lines correctly is the winner. So get set . . . ready . . . go!

1. littleoylue (2) _____

2. ruadudu (3) _____

3. aaaalacksheep (3) _____

4. lowwindlow (2) _____

5. owwowwow (1) _____

6. yeayunting (4) _____

7. colercolermendmyshoe (4) _____

8. hotcrossunshotcrossuns (2) _____

9. hushayeayonthetreetop (3) _____

10. ladyirdladyird (2) _____

"B" is for Baby

By adding B's to the letters below, you will create first lines of well-known Mother Goose Rhymes. Each sequence of letters ends with the number of B's required. The first guest to fill in all the lines correctly is the winner. So get set . . . ready . . . go!

1. littleoylue (2) _____

2. ruadudu (3) _____

3. aaaalacksheep (3) _____

4. lowwindlow (2) _____

5. owwowwow (1) _____

6. yeayunting (4) _____

7. colercolermendmyshoe (4) _____

8. hotcrossunshotcrossuns (2) _____

9. hushayeayonthetreetop (3) _____

10. ladyirdladyird (2) _____

"B" is for Baby

By adding B's to the letters below, you will create first lines of well-known Mother Goose Rhymes. Each sequence of letters ends with the number of B's required. The first guest to fill in all the lines correctly is the winner. So get set . . . ready . . . go!

1. littleoylue (2) _____

2. ruadudu (3) _____

3. aaaalacksheep (3) _____

4. lowwindlow (2) _____

5. owwowwow (1) _____

6. yeayunting (4) _____

7. colercolermendmyshoe (4)_____

8. hotcrossunshotcrossuns (2) _____

9. hushayeayonthetreetop (3) _____

10. ladyirdladyird (2) _____

"B" is for Baby

By adding B's to the letters below, you will create first lines of well-known Mother Goose Rhymes. Each sequence of letters ends with the number of B's required. The first guest to fill in all the lines correctly is the winner. So get set . . . ready . . . go!

1. littleoylue (2) _____

2. ruadudu (3) _____

3. aaaalacksheep (3) _____

4. lowwindlow (2) _____

5. owwowwow (1) _____

6. yeayunting (4) _____

7. colercolermendmyshoe (4) _____

8. hotcrossunshotcrossuns (2) _____

9. hushayeayonthetreetop (3) _____

10. ladyirdladyird (2) _____

What's Your Parenting IQ?

How do you compare with the experts? Here's a chance to show off your parenting knowledge and perhaps learn something new.

If you answer six of these eight questions correctly, you're better informed than most on this subject. All eight answers right? You're "cheaper by the dozen" material!

1. A young child sees the world much as her parents do.
   True/False

2. Children's artwork reveals much about themselves, even though it looks like nothing but scribbles.   True/False

3. A certain amount of crying is perfectly normal.
   True/False

4. Children delight in fairy tales and really are not afraid of the wicked witch.   True/False

5. Stimulation in the form of exciting sounds, sights, and movements is good for baby, while quiet gives the baby nothing.   True/False

6. Ignoring a cranky child is the quickest way to tell him his behavior is unacceptable.   True/False

7. The "terrible twos" stage is the most difficult for parents to get through.   True/False

8. Baby's looks, movements, gestures, and even body posture have meaning.   True/False

What's Your Parenting IQ?

How do you compare with the experts? Here's a chance to show off your parenting knowledge and perhaps learn something new.

If you answer six of these eight questions correctly, you're better informed than most on this subject. All eight answers right? You're "cheaper by the dozen" material!

1. A young child sees the world much as her parents do.
   True/False

2. Children's artwork reveals much about themselves, even though it looks like nothing but scribbles.   True/False

3. A certain amount of crying is perfectly normal.
   True/False

4. Children delight in fairy tales and really are not afraid of the wicked witch.   True/False

5. Stimulation in the form of exciting sounds, sights, and movements is good for baby, while quiet gives the baby nothing.   True/False

6. Ignoring a cranky child is the quickest way to tell him his behavior is unacceptable.   True/False

7. The "terrible twos" stage is the most difficult for parents to get through.   True/False

8. Baby's looks, movements, gestures, and even body posture have meaning.   True/False

What's Your Parenting IQ?

How do you compare with the experts? Here's a chance to show off your parenting knowledge and perhaps learn something new.

If you answer six of these eight questions correctly, you're better informed than most on this subject. All eight answers right? You're "cheaper by the dozen" material!

1. A young child sees the world much as her parents do.
   True/False

2. Children's artwork reveals much about themselves, even though it looks like nothing but scribbles.   True/False

3. A certain amount of crying is perfectly normal.
   True/False

4. Children delight in fairy tales and really are not afraid of the wicked witch.   True/False

5. Stimulation in the form of exciting sounds, sights, and movements is good for baby, while quiet gives the baby nothing.   True/False

6. Ignoring a cranky child is the quickest way to tell him his behavior is unacceptable.   True/False

7. The "terrible twos" stage is the most difficult for parents to get through.   True/False

8. Baby's looks, movements, gestures, and even body posture have meaning.   True/False

What's Your Parenting IQ?

How do you compare with the experts? Here's a chance to show off your parenting knowledge and perhaps learn something new.

If you answer six of these eight questions correctly, you're better informed than most on this subject. All eight answers right? You're "cheaper by the dozen" material!

1. A young child sees the world much as her parents do.
   True/False

2. Children's artwork reveals much about themselves, even though it looks like nothing but scribbles.   True/False

3. A certain amount of crying is perfectly normal.
   True/False

4. Children delight in fairy tales and really are not afraid of the wicked witch.   True/False

5. Stimulation in the form of exciting sounds, sights, and movements is good for baby, while quiet gives the baby nothing.   True/False

6. Ignoring a cranky child is the quickest way to tell him his behavior is unacceptable.   True/False

7. The "terrible twos" stage is the most difficult for parents to get through.   True/False

8. Baby's looks, movements, gestures, and even body posture have meaning.   True/False

What's Your Parenting IQ?

How do you compare with the experts? Here's a chance to show off your parenting knowledge and perhaps learn something new.

If you answer six of these eight questions correctly, you're better informed than most on this subject. All eight answers right? You're "cheaper by the dozen" material!

1. A young child sees the world much as her parents do.
   True/False

2. Children's artwork reveals much about themselves, even though it looks like nothing but scribbles.   True/False

3. A certain amount of crying is perfectly normal.
   True/False

4. Children delight in fairy tales and really are not afraid of the wicked witch.   True/False

5. Stimulation in the form of exciting sounds, sights, and movements is good for baby, while quiet gives the baby nothing.   True/False

6. Ignoring a cranky child is the quickest way to tell him his behavior is unacceptable.   True/False

7. The "terrible twos" stage is the most difficult for parents to get through.   True/False

8. Baby's looks, movements, gestures, and even body posture have meaning.   True/False

What's Your Parenting IQ?

How do you compare with the experts? Here's a chance to show off your parenting knowledge and perhaps learn something new.

If you answer six of these eight questions correctly, you're better informed than most on this subject. All eight answers right? You're "cheaper by the dozen" material!

1. A young child sees the world much as her parents do.
   True/False

2. Children's artwork reveals much about themselves, even though it looks like nothing but scribbles.   True/False

3. A certain amount of crying is perfectly normal.
   True/False

4. Children delight in fairy tales and really are not afraid of the wicked witch.   True/False

5. Stimulation in the form of exciting sounds, sights, and movements is good for baby, while quiet gives the baby nothing.   True/False

6. Ignoring a cranky child is the quickest way to tell him his behavior is unacceptable.   True/False

7. The "terrible twos" stage is the most difficult for parents to get through.   True/False

8. Baby's looks, movements, gestures, and even body posture have meaning.   True/False

What's Your Parenting IQ?

How do you compare with the experts? Here's a chance to show off your parenting knowledge and perhaps learn something new.

If you answer six of these eight questions correctly, you're better informed than most on this subject. All eight answers right? You're "cheaper by the dozen" material!

1. A young child sees the world much as her parents do.
   True/False

2. Children's artwork reveals much about themselves, even though it looks like nothing but scribbles.   True/False

3. A certain amount of crying is perfectly normal.
   True/False

4. Children delight in fairy tales and really are not afraid of the wicked witch.   True/False

5. Stimulation in the form of exciting sounds, sights, and movements is good for baby, while quiet gives the baby nothing.   True/False

6. Ignoring a cranky child is the quickest way to tell him his behavior is unacceptable.   True/False

7. The "terrible twos" stage is the most difficult for parents to get through.   True/False

8. Baby's looks, movements, gestures, and even body posture have meaning.   True/False

What's Your Parenting IQ?

How do you compare with the experts? Here's a chance to show off your parenting knowledge and perhaps learn something new.

If you answer six of these eight questions correctly, you're better informed than most on this subject. All eight answers right? You're "cheaper by the dozen" material!

1. A young child sees the world much as her parents do.
   True/False

2. Children's artwork reveals much about themselves, even though it looks like nothing but scribbles.   True/False

3. A certain amount of crying is perfectly normal.
   True/False

4. Children delight in fairy tales and really are not afraid of the wicked witch.   True/False

5. Stimulation in the form of exciting sounds, sights, and movements is good for baby, while quiet gives the baby nothing.   True/False

6. Ignoring a cranky child is the quickest way to tell him his behavior is unacceptable.   True/False

7. The "terrible twos" stage is the most difficult for parents to get through.   True/False

8. Baby's looks, movements, gestures, and even body posture have meaning.   True/False

What's Your Parenting IQ?

How do you compare with the experts? Here's a chance to show off your parenting knowledge and perhaps learn something new.

If you answer six of these eight questions correctly, you're better informed than most on this subject. All eight answers right? You're "cheaper by the dozen" material!

1. A young child sees the world much as her parents do.
   True/False
2. Children's artwork reveals much about themselves, even though it looks like nothing but scribbles.   True/False
3. A certain amount of crying is perfectly normal.
   True/False
4. Children delight in fairy tales and really are not afraid of the wicked witch.   True/False
5. Stimulation in the form of exciting sounds, sights, and movements is good for baby, while quiet gives the baby nothing.   True/False
6. Ignoring a cranky child is the quickest way to tell him his behavior is unacceptable.   True/False
7. The "terrible twos" stage is the most difficult for parents to get through.   True/False
8. Baby's looks, movements, gestures, and even body posture have meaning.   True/False

What's Your Parenting IQ?

How do you compare with the experts? Here's a chance to show off your parenting knowledge and perhaps learn something new.

If you answer six of these eight questions correctly, you're better informed than most on this subject. All eight answers right? You're "cheaper by the dozen" material!

1. A young child sees the world much as her parents do.
   True/False

2. Children's artwork reveals much about themselves, even though it looks like nothing but scribbles.   True/False

3. A certain amount of crying is perfectly normal.
   True/False

4. Children delight in fairy tales and really are not afraid of the wicked witch.   True/False

5. Stimulation in the form of exciting sounds, sights, and movements is good for baby, while quiet gives the baby nothing.   True/False

6. Ignoring a cranky child is the quickest way to tell him his behavior is unacceptable.   True/False

7. The "terrible twos" stage is the most difficult for parents to get through.   True/False

8. Baby's looks, movements, gestures, and even body posture have meaning.   True/False

What's Your Parenting IQ?

How do you compare with the experts? Here's a chance to show off your parenting knowledge and perhaps learn something new.

If you answer six of these eight questions correctly, you're better informed than most on this subject. All eight answers right? You're "cheaper by the dozen" material!

1. A young child sees the world much as her parents do.
   True/False

2. Children's artwork reveals much about themselves, even though it looks like nothing but scribbles.   True/False

3. A certain amount of crying is perfectly normal.
   True/False

4. Children delight in fairy tales and really are not afraid of the wicked witch.   True/False

5. Stimulation in the form of exciting sounds, sights, and movements is good for baby, while quiet gives the baby nothing.   True/False

6. Ignoring a cranky child is the quickest way to tell him his behavior is unacceptable.   True/False

7. The "terrible twos" stage is the most difficult for parents to get through.   True/False

8. Baby's looks, movements, gestures, and even body posture have meaning.   True/False

What's Your Parenting IQ?

How do you compare with the experts? Here's a chance to show off your parenting knowledge and perhaps learn something new.

If you answer six of these eight questions correctly, you're better informed than most on this subject. All eight answers right? You're "cheaper by the dozen" material!

1. A young child sees the world much as her parents do.
   True/False

2. Children's artwork reveals much about themselves, even though it looks like nothing but scribbles.   True/False

3. A certain amount of crying is perfectly normal.
   True/False

4. Children delight in fairy tales and really are not afraid of the wicked witch.   True/False

5. Stimulation in the form of exciting sounds, sights, and movements is good for baby, while quiet gives the baby nothing.   True/False

6. Ignoring a cranky child is the quickest way to tell him his behavior is unacceptable.   True/False

7. The "terrible twos" stage is the most difficult for parents to get through.   True/False

8. Baby's looks, movements, gestures, and even body posture have meaning.   True/False

Guess Baby's Fortune!

Everyone wants the best of all worlds for the new baby. For baby to succeed, these qualities will be helpful. Sharpen your wand, fill in the missing letters, and the means for making dreams come true will appear. A prize goes to the player who can guess the most good fortune for baby!

You'll find a clue before each word.

1. Rhymes with healthy. __ E __ L T __ __
2. Full of questions. __ __ Q __ __ S __ T __ __ E
3. Scarecrow yearnings. __ __ S D __ __
4. Source of support. __ R __ E __ __ S __ __ __ __
5. It brings smiles. H __ __ __ __ __ N E S S
6. Stems from inspiration. __ __ E __ T __ __ __ __ T __
7. Trust your_____. __ __ T __ __ T __ __ N
8. Brer Rabbit was this. R E S __ __ __ __ __ E F __ L
9. What do presidents, queens, and band majors have in common? L E __ D E R S __ __ __ __
10. Why the turtle won the race. __ E R S __ S T E __ __ __ E
11. _____ of a lion. __ __ __ __ R __ G E
12. The best possible vision. O __ T __ __ __ __ S __
13. A desirable quality in men and women alike. S E __ S __ T __ __ __ __ T __
14. Positive anticipation. E __ T __ __ __ S __ __ __ __ M
15. Laugh and the world laughs with you. H __ __ __ __ R
16. Openhanded. __ E N E R __ __ S

Guess Baby's Fortune!

Everyone wants the best of all worlds for the new baby. For baby to succeed, these qualities will be helpful. Sharpen your wand, fill in the missing letters, and the means for making dreams come true will appear. A prize goes to the player who can guess the most good fortune for baby!

You'll find a clue before each word.

1. Rhymes with healthy. __ E __ L T __ __
2. Full of questions. __ __ Q __ __ S __ T __ __ E
3. Scarecrow yearnings. __ __ S D __ __
4. Source of support. __ R __ E __ __ S __ __ __ __
5. It brings smiles. H __ __ __ __ __ N E S S
6. Stems from inspiration. __ __ E __ T __ __ __ __ T __
7. Trust your_____. __ __ __ T __ __ T __ __ N
8. Brer Rabbit was this. R E S __ __ __ __ __ E F __ L
9. What do presidents, queens, and band majors have in common? L E __ D E R S __ __ __ __
10. Why the turtle won the race. __ E R S __ S T E __ __ E
11. _____ of a lion. __ __ __ __ R __ G E
12. The best possible vision. O __ T __ __ __ __ S __
13. A desirable quality in men and women alike. S E __ S __ T __ __ __ __ T __
14. Positive anticipation. E __ T __ __ S __ __ __ __ M
15. Laugh and the world laughs with you. H __ __ __ __ R
16. Openhanded. __ E N E R __ __ S

Guess Baby's Fortune!

Everyone wants the best of all worlds for the new baby. For baby to succeed, these qualities will be helpful. Sharpen your wand, fill in the missing letters, and the means for making dreams come true will appear. A prize goes to the player who can guess the most good fortune for baby!

You'll find a clue before each word.

1. Rhymes with healthy. __ E __ L T __ __
2. Full of questions. __ __ Q __ __ S __ T __ __ E
3. Scarecrow yearnings. __ __ S D __ __
4. Source of support. __ R __ E __ __ S __ __ __ __
5. It brings smiles. H __ __ __ __ __ N E S S
6. Stems from inspiration. __ __ E __ T __ __ __ __ T __
7. Trust your_____. __ __ T __ __ T __ __ N
8. Brer Rabbit was this. R E S __ __ __ __ __ E F __ L
9. What do presidents, queens, and band majors have in common? L E __ D E R S __ __ __ __
10. Why the turtle won the race. __ E R S __ S T E __ __ E
11. _____ of a lion. __ __ __ R __ G E
12. The best possible vision. O __ T __ __ __ __ S __
13. A desirable quality in men and women alike. S E __ S __ T __ __ __ T __
14. Positive anticipation. E __ T __ __ S __ __ __ M
15. Laugh and the world laughs with you. H __ __ __ __ R
16. Openhanded. __ E N E R __ __ S

Guess Baby's Fortune!

Everyone wants the best of all worlds for the new baby. For baby to succeed, these qualities will be helpful. Sharpen your wand, fill in the missing letters, and the means for making dreams come true will appear. A prize goes to the player who can guess the most good fortune for baby!

You'll find a clue before each word.

1. Rhymes with healthy. __ E __ L T __ __
2. Full of questions. __ __ Q __ __ S __ T __ __ E
3. Scarecrow yearnings. __ __ S D __ __
4. Source of support. __ R __ E __ __ S __ __ __
5. It brings smiles. H __ __ __ __ N E S S
6. Stems from inspiration. __ __ E __ T __ __ __ T __
7. Trust your_____. __ __ T __ __ T __ __ N
8. Brer Rabbit was this. R E S __ __ __ __ __ E F __ L
9. What do presidents, queens, and band majors have in common? L E __ D E R S __ __ __
10. Why the turtle won the race. __ E R S __ S T E __ __ E
11. _____ of a lion. __ __ __ R __ G E
12. The best possible vision. O __ T __ __ __ S __
13. A desirable quality in men and women alike. S E __ S __ T __ __ __ __ T __
14. Positive anticipation. E __ T __ __ S __ __ __ M
15. Laugh and the world laughs with you. H __ __ __ R
16. Openhanded. __ E N E R __ __ S

© 1987, BRIGHTON PUBLICATIONS, INC.

Guess Baby's Fortune!

Everyone wants the best of all worlds for the new baby. For baby to succeed, these qualities will be helpful. Sharpen your wand, fill in the missing letters, and the means for making dreams come true will appear. A prize goes to the player who can guess the most good fortune for baby!

You'll find a clue before each word.

1. Rhymes with healthy. __ E __ L T __ __
2. Full of questions. __ __ Q __ __ S __ T __ __ E
3. Scarecrow yearnings. __ __ S D __ __
4. Source of support. __ R __ E __ __ S __ __ __
5. It brings smiles. H __ __ __ __ N E S S
6. Stems from inspiration. __ __ E __ T __ __ __ T __
7. Trust your_____. __ __ T __ __ T __ __ N
8. Brer Rabbit was this. R E S·__ __ __ __ __ E F __ L
9. What do presidents, queens, and band majors have in common? L E __ D E R S __ __ __
10. Why the turtle won the race. __ E R S __ S T E __ __ E
11. _____ of a lion. __ __ __ __ R __ G E
12. The best possible vision. O __ T __ __ __ S __
13. A desirable quality in men and women alike. S E __ S __ T __ __ __ T __
14. Positive anticipation. E __ T __ __ S __ __ __ M
15. Laugh and the world laughs with you. H __ __ __ R
16. Openhanded. __ E N E R __ __ S

Guess Baby's Fortune!

Everyone wants the best of all worlds for the new baby. For baby to succeed, these qualities will be helpful. Sharpen your wand, fill in the missing letters, and the means for making dreams come true will appear. A prize goes to the player who can guess the most good fortune for baby!

You'll find a clue before each word.

1. Rhymes with healthy. __ E __ L T __ __
2. Full of questions. __ __ Q __ __ S __ T __ __ E
3. Scarecrow yearnings. __ __ S D __ __
4. Source of support. __ R __ E __ __ S __ __ __
5. It brings smiles. H __ __ __ __ N E S S
6. Stems from inspiration. __ __ E __ T __ __ __ T __
7. Trust your_____. __ __ T __ __ T __ __ N
8. Brer Rabbit was this. R E S __ __ __ __ __ E F __ L
9. What do presidents, queens, and band majors have in common? L E __ D E R S __ __ __
10. Why the turtle won the race. __ E R S __ S T E __ __ E
11. _____ of a lion. __ __ __ __ R __ G E
12. The best possible vision. O __ T __ __ __ S __
13. A desirable quality in men and women alike. S E __ S __ T __ __ __ T __
14. Positive anticipation. E __ T __ __ S __ __ __ M
15. Laugh and the world laughs with you. H __ __ __ __ R
16. Openhanded. __ E N E R __ __ S

Guess Baby's Fortune!

Everyone wants the best of all worlds for the new baby. For baby to succeed, these qualities will be helpful. Sharpen your wand, fill in the missing letters, and the means for making dreams come true will appear. A prize goes to the player who can guess the most good fortune for baby!

You'll find a clue before each word.

1. Rhymes with healthy. __ E __ L T __ __
2. Full of questions. __ __ Q __ __ S __ T __ __ E
3. Scarecrow yearnings. __ __ S D __ __
4. Source of support. __ R __ E __ __ S __ __ __
5. It brings smiles. H __ __ __ __ N E S S
6. Stems from inspiration. __ __ E __ T __ __ __ T __
7. Trust your_____. __ __ T __ __ T __ __ N
8. Brer Rabbit was this. R E S __ __ __ __ __ E F __ L
9. What do presidents, queens, and band majors have in common? L E __ D E R S __ __ __ __
10. Why the turtle won the race. __ E R S __ S T E __ __ E
11. _____ of a lion. __ __ __ __ R __ G E
12. The best possible vision. O __ T __ __ __ S __
13. A desirable quality in men and women alike. S E __ S __ T __ __ __ T __
14. Positive anticipation. E __ T __ __ S __ __ __ M
15. Laugh and the world laughs with you. H __ __ __ R
16. Openhanded. __ E N E R __ __ S

Guess Baby's Fortune!

Everyone wants the best of all worlds for the new baby. For baby to succeed, these qualities will be helpful. Sharpen your wand, fill in the missing letters, and the means for making dreams come true will appear. A prize goes to the player who can guess the most good fortune for baby!

You'll find a clue before each word.

1. Rhymes with healthy. __ E __ L T __ __
2. Full of questions. __ __ Q __ __ S __ T __ __ E
3. Scarecrow yearnings. __ __ S D __ __
4. Source of support. __ R __ E __ __ S __ __ __
5. It brings smiles. H __ __ __ __ N E S S
6. Stems from inspiration. __ __ E __ T __ __ __ T __
7. Trust your_____. __ __ T __ __ T __ __ N
8. Brer Rabbit was this. R E S __ __ __ __ __ E F __ L
9. What do presidents, queens, and band majors have in common? L E __ D E R S __ __ __
10. Why the turtle won the race. __ E R S __ S T E __ __ E
11. _____ of a lion. __ __ __ __ R __ G E
12. The best possible vision. O __ T __ __ __ S __
13. A desirable quality in men and women alike.
    S E __ S __ T __ __ __ T __
14. Positive anticipation. E __ T __ __ S __ __ __ M
15. Laugh and the world laughs with you. H __ __ __ R
16. Openhanded. __ E N E R __ __ S

Guess Baby's Fortune!

Everyone wants the best of all worlds for the new baby. For baby to succeed, these qualities will be helpful. Sharpen your wand, fill in the missing letters, and the means for making dreams come true will appear. A prize goes to the player who can guess the most good fortune for baby!

You'll find a clue before each word.

1. Rhymes with healthy. __ E __ L T __ __

2. Full of questions. __ __ Q __ __ S __ T __ __ E

3. Scarecrow yearnings. __ __ S D __ __

4. Source of support. __ R __ E __ __ S __ __ __

5. It brings smiles. H __ __ __ __ N E S S

6. Stems from inspiration. __ __ E __ T __ __ __ T __

7. Trust your_____. __ __ T __ __ T __ __ N

8. Brer Rabbit was this. R E S __ __ __ __ E F __ L

9. What do presidents, queens, and band majors have in common? L E __ D E R S __ __ __

10. Why the turtle won the race. __ E R S __ S T E __ __ E

11. _____ of a lion. __ __ __ R __ G E

12. The best possible vision. O __ T __ __ __ S __

13. A desirable quality in men and women alike. S E __ S __ T __ __ __ T __

14. Positive anticipation. E __ T __ __ S __ __ __ M

15. Laugh and the world laughs with you. H __ __ __ R

16. Openhanded. __ E N E R __ __ S

Guess Baby's Fortune!

Everyone wants the best of all worlds for the new baby. For baby to succeed, these qualities will be helpful. Sharpen your wand, fill in the missing letters, and the means for making dreams come true will appear. A prize goes to the player who can guess the most good fortune for baby!

You'll find a clue before each word.

1. Rhymes with healthy. __ E __ L T __ __
2. Full of questions. __ __ Q __ __ S __ T __ __ E
3. Scarecrow yearnings. __ __ S D __ __
4. Source of support. __ R __ E __ __ S __ __ __
5. It brings smiles. H __ __ __ __ N E S S
6. Stems from inspiration. __ __ E __ T __ __ __ T __
7. Trust your_____. __ __ T __ __ T __ __ N
8. Brer Rabbit was this. R E S __ __ __ __ __ E F __ L
9. What do presidents, queens, and band majors have in common? L E __ D E R S __ __ __
10. Why the turtle won the race. __ E R S __ S T E __ __ E
11. _____ of a lion. __ __ __ R __ G E
12. The best possible vision. O __ T __ __ __ S __
13. A desirable quality in men and women alike. S E __ S __ T __ __ __ T __
14. Positive anticipation. E __ T __ __ S __ __ __ M
15. Laugh and the world laughs with you. H __ __ __ R
16. Openhanded. __ E N E R __ __ S

Guess Baby's Fortune!

Everyone wants the best of all worlds for the new baby. For baby to succeed, these qualities will be helpful. Sharpen your wand, fill in the missing letters, and the means for making dreams come true will appear. A prize goes to the player who can guess the most good fortune for baby!

You'll find a clue before each word.

1. Rhymes with healthy. __ E __ L T __ __
2. Full of questions. __ __ Q __ __ S __ T __ __ E
3. Scarecrow yearnings. __ __ S D __ __
4. Source of support. __ R __ E __ __ S __ __ __
5. It brings smiles. H __ __ __ __ N E S S
6. Stems from inspiration. __ __ E __ T __ __ __ T __
7. Trust your_____. __ __ T __ __ T __ __ N
8. Brer Rabbit was this. R E S __ __ __ __ __ E F __ L
9. What do presidents, queens, and band majors have in common? L E __ D E R S __ __ __
10. Why the turtle won the race. __ E R S __ S T E __ __ E
11. _____ of a lion. __ __ __ R __ G E
12. The best possible vision. O __ T __ __ __ S __
13. A desirable quality in men and women alike.
    S E __ S __ T __ __ __ T __
14. Positive anticipation. E __ T __ __ S __ __ __ M
15. Laugh and the world laughs with you. H __ __ __ R
16. Openhanded. __ E N E R __ __ S

Guess Baby's Fortune!

Everyone wants the best of all worlds for the new baby. For baby to succeed, these qualities will be helpful. Sharpen your wand, fill in the missing letters, and the means for making dreams come true will appear. A prize goes to the player who can guess the most good fortune for baby!

You'll find a clue before each word.

1. Rhymes with healthy. __ E __ L T __ __
2. Full of questions. __ __ Q __ __ S __ T __ __ E
3. Scarecrow yearnings. __ __ S D __ __
4. Source of support. __ R __ E __ __ S __ __ __
5. It brings smiles. H __ __ __ __ N E S S
6. Stems from inspiration. __ __ E __ T __ __ __ T __
7. Trust your_____. __ __ T __ __ T __ __ N
8. Brer Rabbit was this. R E S __ __ __ __ __ E F __ L
9. What do presidents, queens, and band majors have in common? L E __ D E R S __ __ __
10. Why the turtle won the race. __ E R S __ S T E __ __ E
11. _____ of a lion. __ __ __ R __ G E
12. The best possible vision. O __ T __ __ __ S __
13. A desirable quality in men and women alike. S E __ S __ T __ __ __ T __
14. Positive anticipation. E __ T __ __ S __ __ __ M
15. Laugh and the world laughs with you. H __ __ __ R
16. Openhanded. __ E N E R __ __ S

© 1987, BRIGHTON PUBLICATIONS, INC.

Name Tag Patterns

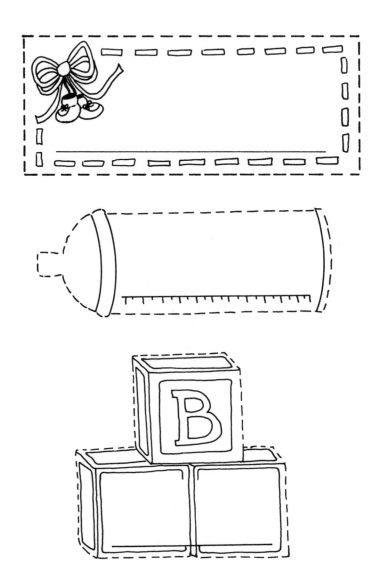

Name Tag Patterns

Name Tag Patterns

Answers to Ready-To-Use Games

Famous Baby Trivia

1. Bambi
2. Pebbles
3. Marvin
4. Moses
5. Dumplings
6. Dumbo
7. "Rosemary's Baby"
8. New Year's Baby
9. Ugly Duckling
10. Sparkle Plenty
11. Baby Bear
12. "Whatever Happened to Baby Jane?"
13. Rockabye Baby
14. Sweet Pea
15. Charmin Baby

"B" is for Baby

1. Little boy blue
2. Rub-a-dub-dub
3. Baa, baa, black sheep
4. Blow, wind, blow!
5. Bow, wow, wow
6. Bye, baby bunting
7. Cobbler, cobbler, mend my shoe
8. Hot cross buns, hot cross buns
9. Hush-a-bye, baby, on the tree top
10. Ladybird, ladybird

What's Your Parenting IQ?

1. False. The world is seen very differently from a child's viewpoint. Adults seem enormous because of the child's small size. A good exercise: get down on your hands and knees for awhile for a child's perspective of the world.

2. True. From scribbles to self-portraits, researchers have found that children reflect their changing physical mastery and view of the world through their artwork.

3. True. Some experts even believe that a particularly fussy day may indicate the beginning of a new developmental stage.

4. True. Children delight in the same fairy tales that were a part of your childhood. By the time children are five or six years old, their experience in the real world teaches them that fairy tales aren't real.

5. False. New research has shown that quiet times in the form of slow, rhythmic body movements and receptive facial expressions are important as well. Babies find it easier to focus on and stay interested in the calmer expressions.

6. False. The experts say the best way to handle a sulky child is to acknowledge what he is feeling while clearly defining acceptable behavior.

7. False. As it turns out, each age offers its share of difficulties. It all depends on the parent. How difficult a child is at any one age depends a great deal on the parent's own idiosyncracies.

8. True. Videotape technology has now shown that even a two- or three-week-old reveals herself to possess a behavior language.

Guess Baby's Fortune!

1. WEALTHY
2. INQUISITIVE
3. WISDOM
4. FRIENDSHIP
5. HAPPINESS
6. CREATIVITY
7. INTUITION
8. RESOURCEFUL
9. LEADERSHIP
10 PERSISTENCE
11. COURAGE
12. OPTIMISM
13. SENSITIVITY
14. ENTHUSIASM
15. HUMOR
16. GENEROUS

112

Available from Brighton Publications, Inc.

Baby Shower Fun by Sharon Dlugosch

Games for Baby Shower Fun by Sharon Dlugosch

Kid-Tastic Birthday Parties: The Complete Party Planner for Today's Kids by Jane Chase

Romantic At-Home Dinners: Sneaky Strategies for Couples with Kids by Nan Booth/Gary Fischler

Games for Wedding Shower Fun by Sharon Dlugosch/Florence Nelson

Wedding Plans: 50 Unique Themes for the Wedding of Your Dreams by Sharon Dlugosch

Wedding Hints & Reminders by Sharon Dlugosch

Wedding Occasions: 101 New Party Themes for Wedding Showers, Rehearsal Dinners, Engagement Parties, and More! by Cynthia Lueck Sowden

Dream Weddings Do Come True: How to Plan a Stress-free Wedding by Cynthia Kreuger

Reunions for Fun-Loving Families by Nancy Funke Bagley

An Anniversary to Remember: Years One to Seventy-five by Cynthia Lueck Sowden

Folding Table Napkins: A New Look at a Traditional Craft by Sharon Dlugosch

Table Setting Guide by Sharon Dlugosch

Tabletop Vignettes by Sharon Dlugosch

Don't Slurp Your Soup: A Basic Guide to Business Etiquette by Betty Craig

Hit the Ground Running: Communicate Your Way to Success by Cynthia Kreuger

These books are available in selected stores and catalogs. If you're having trouble finding them in your area, send a self-addressed, stamped, business-size envelope and request ordering information from:

Brighton Publications, Inc.
P.O. Box 120706
St. Paul, MN 55112-0706

or call: 1-800-536-BOOK